Final Accounts for Sole Traders and Partnerships
Wise Guide

Image of owl © Eric Isselée-Fotolia.com

Published by Osborne Books Limited, Unit 1B Everoak Estate, Bromyard Road, Worcester WR2 5HP
Tel 01905 748071, Email books@osbornebooks.co.uk, Website www.osbornebooks.co.uk

Printed and bound by Mimeo, UK.

ISBN 978 1909173 439

how to use this Wise Guide

This Wise Guide has been designed to supplement your Tutorial and Workbook. It has two main aims:

- to reinforce your learning as you study your course
- to help you prepare for your online assessment

This Wise Guide is organised in the specific topic areas listed on pages 4 and 5. These individual topic areas have been designed to cover the main areas of study, concentrating on specific areas of difficulty. There is also an index at the back to help you find the areas you are studying or revising.

The Owl symbolises wisdom, and acts as your tutor, introducing and explaining topics. Please let us know if he is doing his job properly. If you have feedback on this material please email books@osbornebooks.co.uk

Thank you and good luck with your study and revision.

Osborne Books

REVISION TIPS

'OWL' stands for: **O**bserve **W**rite **L**earn

There are a number of well-known ways in which you can remember information:

■ *You can remember what it looks like on the page. Diagrams, lists, mind-maps, colour coding for different types of information, all help you **observe** and remember.*

■ *You can remember what you **write** down. Flash cards, post-it notes around the bathroom mirror, notes on a mobile phone all help. It is the process of writing which fixes the information in the brain.*

■ *You can **learn** by using this Wise Guide. Read through each topic carefully and then prepare your own written version on flash cards, post-it notes, wall charts – anything that you can see regularly.*

■ *Lastly, give yourself **chill out** time, your brain a chance to recover and the information time to sink in. Promise yourself treats when you have finished studying – a drink, chocolate, a work out. Relax! And pass.*

list of contents

INTRODUCTION

The trial balance is a list of all account balances in the general ledger. It is the original source of data for producing the financial statements.

The account balances in the trial balance are grouped into those that are entered in the statement of profit or loss and those that are entered in the statement of financial position.

things to remember about the trial balance:

- some of the balances in the **initial trial balance** are modified for period-end adjustments before being entered in the financial statements

- errors which result in the trial balance failing to balance should be corrected by journal before drawing up the financial statements, but note that the trial balance does not reveal all errors in the double-entry bookkeeping

- the final modified and corrected trial balance used for the transfer of balances to the financial statements is the **extended trial balance**

errors revealed by the trial balance

The next three pages illustrate errors which can occur in the initial trial balance.

error	description	treatment in journal
one-sided entry	only one side (debit or credit) of the transaction entered	enter the missing entry and post the other side to Suspense
both entries on the same side	instead of a debit and a credit, two debits or two credits have been entered	remove one of the duplicated entries and post the other side to Suspense
entries of different amounts	the debit and credit entries do not balance	remove the incorrect entry, post the other side to Suspense then make the correct entry and post the other side to Suspense
error in balance transfer to Trial Balance	an incorrect balance figure is transferred to the Trial Balance	
balance omitted from Trial Balance	an account balance is not transferred to the Trial Balance	enter the missing balance and post the other side to Suspense

EXAMPLE 1 – the trial balance debit total is higher than the credit total

The debit column of a Trial Balance total is £200,000 and the credit column total is £198,000. There is a difference (imbalance) in value of £2,000 credit.

the following errors would individually create this difference (imbalance):

description	type of error
VAT of £2,000 from the sales day book has not been entered in the VAT account	one-sided entry
a bank payment for rent of £1,000 has been debited both the rent and the bank accounts	both entries on same to side
discount received of £3,000 has been debited to purchases ledger control account as £5,000	unequal entries
accumulated depreciation of £4,200 has been entered in the trial balance as £2,200	error in transfer to trial balance
accrued expenses totalling £2,000 have been debited to the expense account but the accruals entry has not been included in the trial balance	balance omitted from the trial balance

EXAMPLE 2 – the trial balance credit total is higher than the debit total

The debit column of a Trial Balance total is £425,000 and the credit column total is £430,000. There is a difference (imbalance) in value of £5,000 credit.

the following errors would individually create this difference (imbalance):

description	type of error
VAT of £5,000 from the purchases day book has not been entered in the VAT account	one-sided entry
a bank receipt for commission of £2,500 has been credited to both the commission and the bank accounts	both entries on same side
discount allowed of £3,000 has been credited to sales ledger control account as £8,000	unequal entries
a depreciation charge of £9,200 has been entered in the trial balance as £4,200	error in transfer to trial balance
accrued income totalling £5,000 has been credited to the income account but the accruals entry has not been included in the trial balance	balance omitted from the trial balance

balance transfers to the statement of profit or loss (SPL)

The following balances are transferred from the trial balance and end-of-year adjustments:

- ### income accounts
  Sales, interest received, discount received, profit on disposal of non-current assets

- ### day-to-day expenses
  Everyday running costs of the business, eg administration expenses, advertising and promotion, electricity, rent and rates, interest paid, discount allowed

- ### periodic charges or expenses
  Depreciation charges, loss on disposal of non-current assets, irrecoverable debts, allowance for doubtful debts adjustment

- ### cost of sales
  The following balances are transferred as individual amounts and then the following calculation is made within the statement of profit or loss: Cost of sales = Opening inventory + Purchases – Purchases returns – Closing inventory

Notes:
- The calculation of net profit (or loss) is carried out within the statement of profit or loss (SPL) – which works as a double-entry 'T' account – and not in the trial balance.
- The balance of the accounts used to make transfers to the SPL **revert to zero** (apart from accrual and prepayment accounts which still have carried down balances).

balance transfers to the statement of financial position (SFP)

The following amounts are transferred from the trial balance and end-of-year adjustments:

■ **assets**
Non-current assets: carrying amount (or net book value), ie original cost less accumulated depreciation
Current assets: closing inventory, trade receivables (sales ledger control account) less allowance for doubtful debts, insurance claims, prepayment of expenses, accrual of income, cash and cash equivalents (bank and cash)

■ **liabilities**
Current liabilities: trade payables (purchases ledger control account), VAT and other taxes, accrual of expenses, prepayment of income
Non-current liabilities: loans or amounts due for repayment in more than a year

■ **capital**
Opening capital + Capital introduced during the period + Profit generated during the period (or – Loss generated during the period) – Drawings = Closing capital

Note: The SFP is different from the SPL in that it is not a double-entry account: it is only the amounts that are copied over from the trial balance and year-end adjustments. The ledger balances which provide the figures continue on into the next financial period.

An example of an **extended trial balance** is shown on the next two pages.

EXAMPLE: trial balance as at 31 December 20X4

	Dr	Cr	SPL	SFP
Sales		350,000	√	
Sales returns	5,000		√	
Purchases	200,000		√	
Carriage inwards	3,500		√	
Purchases returns		2,500	√	
Advertising	12,000		√	
Administration expenses	13,000		√	
Wages	39,000		√	
Premises expenses	11,500		√	
Discount allowed	3,000		√	
Discount received		2,000	√	
Distribution expenses	4,000		√	
Loan interest	1,100		√	
Depreciation charge	7,000		√	
Loss on disposal of n/c asset	200		√	
Inventory (opening)	75,000		√	
Closing inventory SPL		70,000	√	
Irrecoverable debts	500		√	
Allowance for d/debts adjustment	300		√	

	Dr	Cr	SPL	SFP
Machinery	36,000			√
Accumulated depreciation		14,000		√
Closing inventory SFP	70,000			√
Sales ledger control	30,000			√
Allowance for d/debts		500		√
Prepayments	1,000			√
Bank	9,900			√
Purchases ledger control		20,000		√
VAT		16,000		√
Accruals		1,500		√
Bank loan		21,500		√
Capital		45,000		√
Drawings	21,000			√
Totals	543,000	543,000		

extended trial balance – points to note

■ the SPL and SFP columns are ticked to identify the entries needed for the appropriate financial statement

■ the accounts will sometimes be listed alphabetically – in assessments for example – so you will need to be careful in choosing the correct column to tick

sp

extended trial balance – points to note (continued)

- the trial balance may include lines where both a debit and a credit balance are shown; this means you need to know which entry goes in which financial statement:

	Dr	Cr	SPL	SFP
Closing inventory SFP/SPL	70,000	70,000	√ (Cr)	√ (Dr)
Sales/purchase ledger control	30,000	20,000		√ (Dr) √ (Cr)
Discounts allowed/received	3,000	2,000	√ (Dr) √ (Cr)	

- sometimes account balances may either be added together or 'netted off' (one balance subtracted from the other) when they are transferred to the financial statements:

	Dr	Cr	
Sales		350,000	Sales revenue 345,000
Sales returns	5,000		

	Dr	Cr	
Purchases	200,000		Purchases 203,500
Carriage inwards	3,500		

- the account balances that make up Cost of sales can be transferred from the trial balance to the SPL individually, or they may be combined first in a Cost of sales 'T' account. In this case only the balance of the Cost of sales account is transferred.

year-end adjustments summary – transfers to the financial statements

After period-end adjustments, the revised account balances are transferred as follows:

Adjustment	SPL	SFP
Accrual of income	Add to income	Show as current asset
Accrual of expense	Add to expense	Show as current liability
Prepayment of income	Deduct from income	Show as current liability
Prepayment of expense	Deduct from expense	Show as current asset
Depreciation charge	Show as expense	Increase accumulated dep'n
Irrecoverable debt	Show as expense	Deduct from trade receivables
Allowance for d/debt increase	Show as expense	Reduce trade receivables by ongoing allowance
Allowance for d/debt decrease	Add to income	
Closing inventory	Reduce purchases (in cost of sales)	Show as current asset
Goods for owner use	Add to sales	Add to drawings
Gain on disposal of NCA	Show as income	Non-current assets value reduced by disposal
Loss on disposal of NCA	Show as expense	

INTRODUCTION

It is important that you are able to produce financial statements from incomplete accounting records. You must therefore know how to extract financial information from records which are missing data.
It is also important to be able to recognise situations which may lead to records being incomplete.

reasons why records may be incomplete

- proper accounting records have not been kept with the result that the information available is sketchy, eg there may be just a cash book and bank statements

- data may have been lost through some disaster, eg fire, flood, theft, computer failure

- there are discrepancies within the existing system, eg between inventory records and actual inventory; between purchases ledger balances and supplier statements

- timing differences are not built into the system, eg customer receipts are not matched to outstanding balances at a particular date

what tools, techniques or resources might help?

sources of help	examples of how the sources might help
the accounting equation Assets less Liabilities = Capital	there may be a trial balance and financial statements for the beginning of the period
bank details – statements, paying-in books, cheque stubs	details of bank transactions can be extracted from bank statements even if no cash book is available
mark-ups, margins and VAT	the cost of goods sold can be estimated using the sales value less a percentage
documents – sales and bills for expenses	totals for sales, purchases and purchase invoices, can be calculated from relevant documents
physical count of inventory	closing inventory value can be calculated
control accounts – receivables, payables, VAT	start of period values owing and owed are the starting point for the current year
any existing values	where a value is missing, knowledge of double-entry and simple arithmetic can be used to calculate the figure from existing values

use of control accounts

Control accounts can be used to calculate missing figures in the accounting records.

In the pages that follow are set out examples of missing figures in control accounts for the sales ledger, purchases ledger, VAT and specific expenses.

sales ledger control account – entries

Sales ledger control			
Balance b/d	A	Sales returns	B
Credit sales	C	Payments from customers	D
		Settlement discount allowed	E
		Irrecoverable debts	F
		Contra	G
		Balance c/d	H
	X		X
Balance b/d	H		

Any of the figures represented by the letters A to H can be calculated if all the other figures are known. See the example below.

Also note that where any double-entry account deals with the first period of a new business there will be no balance brought down at the beginning of that period.

Sales ledger control			
Balance b/d	22,500	Sales returns	3,100
Credit sales	155,400	Payments from customers	137,900
		Settlement discount allowed	?
		Irrecoverable debts	700
		Balance c/d	34,000
	177,900		177,900
Balance b/d	34,000		

Settlement discount allowed calculation
In this case it is a credit entry that is missing.

The calculation is:	£
Total of credit side	177,900
less existing credit entries: 3,100 + 137,900 + 700 + 34,000 =	175,700
Settlement discount allowed figure	2,200

purchases ledger control account – entries

Purchases ledger control			
Purchases returns	A	Balance b/d	B
Payments to suppliers	C	Credit purchases	D
Settlement discount rec'd	E		
Contra	F		
Balance c/d	G		
	X		X
		Balance b/d	G

Any of the figures represented by the letters A to G can be calculated if all the other figures are known.

See the example below.

EXAMPLE

Purchases ledger control account – calculation of the missing figure

Purchases ledger control			
Purchases returns	2,300	Balance b/d	31,200
Payments to suppliers	121,600	**Credit purchases**	?
Settlement discount received	400		
Balance c/d	23,600		
	147,900		147,900
		Balance b/d	23,600

Credit purchases calculation

In this case it is a credit entry that is missing.

The calculation is:	£
Total of credit side	147,900
less Balance brought down	31,200
Credit purchases figure	116,700

VAT control account – entries

VAT control			
Sales returns day book	A	Balance b/d	B
Purchases day book	C	Sales day book	D
Cash book cash payments	E	Cash book cash receipts	F
HMRC	G		
Balance c/d	H		
	X		X
		Balance b/d	H

Any of the figures represented by the letters A to H can be calculated if all the other figures are known.

See the example below.

EXAMPLE

VAT control account – calculation of the missing figure

VAT control			
Sales returns day book	2,500	Balance b/d	9,100
Purchases day book	77,600	Sales day book	110,800
Cash book cash expenses	7,400	Cash sales	4,200
Bank	27,300		
Balance c/d	?		
	124,100		**124,100**
		Balance b/d	?

Balance c/d and b/d calculation

In this case it is the final balance to be brought forward that is missing.
The figure appears in the account twice – as a debit (c/d) and as a credit (b/d).
The calculation is based on the normal balancing rules:

	£
Total of both debit and credit sides	124,100
less existing debit entries:	
2,500 + 77,600 + 7,400 + 27,300 =	114,800
Balance c/d and b/d figure	9,300

Expenses control account – entries

It is possible to construct a control account for total expenses or for any particular area of expense, eg administration. Any accruals or prepayments must be included.

Expenses control			
Cash book payments	A	Balance b/d (accrual)	B
Balance c/d (accrual)	D	Statement of profit or loss	C
	X		X
		Balance b/d (accrual)	D

Any of the figures represented by the letters A to D can be calculated if all the other figures are known.

See the example below.

EXAMPLE

Expenses control account – calculation of the missing figure

Expenses control			
Cash book payments	38,200	Balance b/d (accrual)	400
Balance c/d (accrual)	700	**Statement of profit or loss**	?
	38,900		38,900
		Balance b/d (accrual)	700

Calculation of transfer to statement of profit or loss
Here it is a credit figure that is missing.

The calculation is:	£
Total of the credit side	38,900
less opening credit balance:	400
Transfer to SPL figure	38,500

Note: this method can also be used for situations which involve just a prepayment or both accruals and prepayments.

Bank account – entries

Bank (cash book)			
Balance b/d	A	Payments to suppliers (Purchase ledger control account)	B
Receipts from customers (Sales ledger control account)	C	General expenses	D
Cash sale receipts	E	Loan repayments	F
Interest received	G	Purchase of n/c asset	H
Capital introduced	I	Drawings	J
		Balance c/d	K
	X		X
Balance b/d	K		

Although the bank account in the cash book is not a control account, a summary can be produced to help calculate missing figures.

Note:

A debit balance in the cash book of a business represents money in the bank; confusingly, a bank refers to this as a 'credit balance' on the bank statement – this is because this is money owed to the customer and so is a credit balance (payable) in the accounting records of the bank.

A credit balance in the cash book of a business represents a bank overdraft; on the bank statement this is a 'debit balance' as this is money owed by the customer to the bank.

EXAMPLE

Bank account – calculation of the missing figure

Bank (cash book)			
Balance b/d	6,500	Payments to suppliers	75,200
Receipts from customers	97,400	General expenses	8,200
Cash sale receipts	17,300	Loan repayments	3,600
Interest received	100	Purchase of n/c asset	2,900
Balance c/d	5,700	**Drawings**	?
	127,000		127,000
		Balance b/d	5,700

Drawings calculation

In this case it is a credit figure that is missing.

The calculation is:	£
Total of the credit side	127,000
less existing credit entries:	
75,200 + 8,200 + 3,600 + 2,900 =	89,900
Drawings figure	37,100

3 Incomplete records – the accounting equation

INTRODUCTION

An understanding of the workings of the accounting equation can help to fill in gaps when accounting records are incomplete.

It is possible that you will have covered this topic already in your study of the Accounts Preparation Unit. This topic is also important in the Unit covered by this Wise Guide.

the accounting equation

assets	*minus*	**liabilities**	*equals*	**capital**
non-current assets + current assets		non-current liabilities + current liabilities		opening capital + capital introduced + profit – drawings

If you are not familiar with the terminology in the diagram above you should study page 51.

how the accounting equation works

A change in values in any part of the accounting equation may alter the totals, but the equation will always work, as seen below:

Example: a business purchases shop fittings on credit; they cost £5,000 plus VAT. The accounting equation will change as follows:

Assets	minus	Liabilities		equals	Capital
£		£			£
80,000	–	60,000		=	20,000
+ £5,000		+ £6,000	(payables)		
		– 1,000	(VAT)		
85,000	–	65,000		=	20,000

Also, the elements of the accounting equation can be moved around so that any element can be calculated if the other two are known, for example (using the above figures):

example:	capital	plus	liabilities	equals	assets
	£20,000	+	£60,000	=	£80,000

example:	assets	minus	capital	equals	liabilities
	£80,000	–	£20,000	=	£60,000

calculating figures missing in the capital section

The capital section in the statement of financial position summarises movement in owner capital during the period.

The elements (with sample figures) are:

Opening capital £80,000 + **Capital introduced** £20,000 + **Profit for the period** £100,000 *minus* **Drawings** £30,000 *equals* **Closing capital** £170,000.

Where any one figure is missing it can be calculated using simple maths:

Example 1: the Capital introduced figure is missing:

Opening capital		Capital introduced		Profit for the period		Drawings		Closing capital
£80,000	+	**£????**	+	£100,000	–	£30,000	=	£170,000

Workings: £170,000 + £30,000 – £100,000 – £80,000 = Capital introduced is £20,000

Example 2: the Drawings figure is missing:

Opening capital		Capital introduced		Profit for the period		Drawings		Closing capital
£80,000	+	£20,000	+	£100,000	–	**£????**	=	£170,000

Workings: £80,000 + £20,000 + £100,000 – £170,000 = Drawings are £30,000

calculating the capital from asset and liability totals

The capital figures can be calculated from the asset and liability totals – see below.

EXAMPLE 1 – working out the capital figures

The assets and liabilities for a sole trader business at the beginning and end of the year 20X0 are shown below.

	1 Jan 20X0 £	31 Dec 20X0 £
Cleaning equipment and machinery	12,000	15,000
Inventory of materials	38,400	44,700
Trade receivables (customers)	43,800	30,600
Bank balance (money in bank)	10,000	13,000
Total assets	104,200	103,300
Trade payables (suppliers)	31,200	24,000
General expenses owing	2,000	1,000
Bank loan outstanding	18,000	15,000
Total liabilities	51,200	40,000

Using the data in the table on the previous page you can work out the entries in the capital section.

solution: calculating opening capital (1 January 20X0)

Deduct total liabilities from total assets at the beginning of the year to calculate opening capital:

	Total assets	£104,200
minus	Total liabilities	£51,200
equals	Opening capital	£53,000

solution: calculating closing capital (31 December 20X0)

Deduct total liabilities from total assets at the end of the year to calculate closing capital:

	Total assets	£103,300
minus	Total liabilities	£40,000
equals	Closing capital	£63,300

using the capital position to calculate profit

The basic formula for calculating the capital position (assuming no additional capital has been introduced) is as follows:

opening capital *plus* **profit for the period** *minus* **drawings** *equals* **closing capital**

If you know all the figures apart from the profit figure this can be calculated from the other figures. The example that follows uses the capital figures calculated in the previous example to work out the missing figure of profit. Drawings for the year were £20,000.

EXAMPLE 2 – working out the profit

These are the figures you have calculated so far:

	Opening capital	£53,000
plus	Profit (missing figure)	£?????
minus	Drawings	£20,000
equals	Closing capital	£63,300

Profit can then be calculated by re-arranging the formula quoted above:

closing capital *plus* **drawings** *minus* **opening capital** *equals* **profit**

| £63,300 | + | £20,000 | – | £53,000 | = | £30,300 profit |

---

4 Incomplete records – margin and mark-up

STRETCHING THE BRAIN

Possibly the most challenging area of incomplete records is calculating missing figures by using two different approaches to measuring gross profit percentage (or fraction): these are margin and mark-up.

Understanding the difference between these two formulas is crucial to being able to use the two techniques effectively.

definitions

▨ **margin** = gross profit expressed as a percentage (or fraction) of **sales**:

The formula is $\dfrac{\text{gross profit}}{\text{sales price}} \times 100$

▨ **mark-up** = gross profit expressed as a percentage (or fraction) of **cost**:

The formula is $\dfrac{\text{gross profit}}{\text{cost price}} \times 100$

EXAMPLE 1 – margin and mark-up – how they are different

A product which sells for £80 has a cost of £50 and a gross profit of £30.

calculation of margin % in relation to the selling price

The selling price of £80 is made up of a cost of £50 and a margin of £30. The percentages of these two figures in relation to the selling price are:

- ■ cost   (£50 ÷ £80) x 100 = 62.5%
- ■ **margin**   (£30 ÷ £80) x 100 = **37.5%**

calculation of mark-up % in relation to the cost

This percentage calculation is based on the **cost of £50** and so the gross profit mark-up is the amount of £30 added on to reach the selling price:

- ■ cost   (£50 ÷ £50) x 100 = 100%
- ■ **mark-up**   (£30 ÷ £50) x 100 = **60%**

conclusion

In these two examples the cost, profit and selling price are the same, but:

– margin is the percentage of the selling price which is profit

– mark-up is the percentage of the cost which is added on to make a profit

EXAMPLE 2 – margin and mark-up in the gross profit calculation

	£	£
Sales revenue (a)		180,000
Cost of sales:		
Opening inventory (b)	37,500	
Purchases (c)	147,500	
	185,000	
Less Closing inventory (d)	41,000	
Cost of sales (e)		144,000
Gross profit (f)		36,000

Margin is gross profit (f) expressed as a percentage of sales value (a). This is used by accountants and managers to show how much of sales revenue is profit.

Margin is: $\dfrac{36,000}{180,000} \times 100 = \textbf{20\%}$

Mark-up is gross profit (f) expressed as a percentage of cost of sales (e). This is the amount a business adds to the cost of a product to calculate a selling price.

Mark-up is $\dfrac{36,000}{144,000} \times 100 = \textbf{25\%}$

how are margin and mark-up used in incomplete records accounting?

The following missing values can be calculated if all other relevant figures are known and either expected margin or expected mark-up is known.

- sales

- purchases

- opening inventory

- closing inventory

- drawings of goods

- separation of a VAT-inclusive inventory figure into net and VAT

All these values feature in the trading account part of the statement of profit or loss, ie the first part down to the calculation of gross profit.

If there were missing figures in the trading account shown on the previous page, it would be possible to calculate them using the expected margin of 20% and/or the expected mark-up of 25%.

See the example on the next page where the sales revenue figure is missing.

EXAMPLE – calculating the missing sales revenue figure

	£	£
Sales revenue (a)		??????
Cost of sales:		
Opening inventory (b)	37,500	
Purchases (c)	147,500	
	185,000	
Less Closing inventory (d)	41,000	
Cost of sales (e)		144,000
Gross profit (f)		36,000

Using mark-up:

You know that cost of sales is £144,000 and that the mark-up is 25%.

The sales revenue calculation is therefore £144,000 + (144,000 x 25%) = £180,000.

Using margin:

You know that cost of sales is £144,000 and that the margin is 20%.

Cost of sales is 80% of Sales, so Sales revenue = $\frac{£144,000 \times 100}{80}$ = £180,000.

EXAMPLE – calculating the missing purchases and gross profit figures from the margin percentage

	£	£
Sales revenue (a)		180,000
Cost of sales:		
Opening inventory (b)	37,500	
Purchases (c)	?????	
	?????	
Less Closing inventory (d)	41,000	
Cost of sales (e)		?????
Gross profit (f)		?????

- Purchases (c) is missing, so also are Cost of sales (e) and Gross profit (f).

- The margin is 20% (see page 38) so Gross profit is £180,000 x 20% = £36,000.

- Cost of sales equals £180,000 (Sales) – £36,000 (Gross profit) = £144,000.

- Purchases equals Cost of sales + Closing inventory – Opening inventory, ie:
  Purchases equals £144,000 + £41,000 – £37,500 = £147,500.

EXAMPLE – calculating the opening inventory value

	£	£
Sales revenue (a)		180,000
Cost of sales:		
Opening inventory (b)	?????	
Purchases (c)	147,500	
	?????	
Less Closing inventory (d)	41,000	
Cost of sales (e)		?????
Gross profit (f)		?????

■ Opening inventory (b) is missing, so also are Cost of sales (e) and Gross profit (f).

■ The margin is 20% so Gross profit is £180,000 x 20% = £36,000. This figure will enable you to work back to find the opening inventory.

■ Cost of sales equals £180,000 (Sales) – £36,000 (Gross profit) = £144,000.

■ Opening inventory equals Cost of sales + Closing inventory – Purchases, ie:
Opening inventory equals £144,000 + £41,000 – £147,500 = £37,500.

EXAMPLE – calculating the closing inventory value

	£	£
Sales revenue (a)		180,000
Cost of sales:		
Opening inventory (b)	37,500	
Purchases (c)	147,500	
	185,000	
Less Closing inventory (d)	?????	
Cost of sales (e)		?????
Gross profit (f)		?????

■ Closing inventory (d) is missing, so also are Cost of sales (e) and Gross profit (f).

■ The margin is 20% so Gross profit is £180,000 x 20% = £36,000. This figure will enable you to work back to find the closing inventory.

■ Cost of sales equals £180,000 (Sales) – £36,000 (Gross profit) = £144,000.

■ Closing inventory equals Opening inventory + Purchases – Cost of sales, ie: £37,500 + £147,500 – £144,000 = £41,000.

drawings of inventory by the owner

Sometimes the owner of a business may take inventory out of the business (inventory drawings) in addition to the usual money drawings. This taking of inventory – and any loss of inventory such as theft – may go unrecorded and cause a discrepancy. The value of the missing inventory can be calculated using **the expected margin** of the business.

EXAMPLE – calculating the value of inventory taken as business drawings

- the **actual figures** are sales £200,000, opening inventory £20,000, purchases £165,000 and closing inventory £15,000, giving a profit of £30,000

- the **expected margin** of the business is 20%, and so the expected cost of sales will be: £200,000 x (100 – 20)/100 = £160,000 and the profit £40,000

	expected (£)	actual (£)
Sales revenue	200,000	200,000
Opening inventory	20,000	20,000
+ Purchases	165,000	165,000
– *Closing inventory*	*25,000*	*15,000*
= Cost of sales	160,000	170,000
Gross profit margin	20%	15%
Gross profit	40,000	30,000

continued below

- the **expected closing inventory figure** is therefore : opening inventory £20,000 + purchases £165,000 – cost of sales £160,000 = **£25,000**

- the **drawings of inventory** (the value missing) = **expected closing inventory – actual closing inventory,** in this case: **£25,000 – £15,000 = £10,000**

calculation of an inventory value when the total includes VAT

- An inventory total may still include a 'mark-up' of VAT which causes a discrepancy.
- This VAT element will have to be calculated and deducted before the inventory value can be adjusted in the accounts.

EXAMPLE – calculation of 20% VAT content of a 'gross' inventory amount of £120

- **formula method:**

$$\frac{\text{VAT percentage (20)} \times \text{whole amount including VAT (120)}}{100 + \text{VAT percentage (100 + 20)}} = \frac{2,400}{120} = £20$$

- **VAT fraction method using fraction issued by HMRC: 1/6 in the case of 20%**

  For VAT at 20% divide the VAT inclusive amount by 6. In this case £120 ÷ 6 **= £20.** Note that this fraction will change when the VAT rate changes (see HMRC website).

- The amount of inventory to include in the accounts is 120 – 20 = 100

5 Sole trader financial statements

INTRODUCTION

A sole trader is an unincorporated business owned and run by one individual. The owner has complete control and independence but also has unlimited financial responsibility for any debts of the business.

*Profitability is measured by drawing up the **statement of profit or loss** in a set format. A summary of the assets and liabilities of the business is given in the **statement of financial position**.*

drawing up the statement of profit or loss (SPL)

- the source of the figures for the statement of profit or loss is:
  - the initial trial balance (ITB) or extended trial balance (ETB)
  - the end-of-period adjustments
- the figures are set out in the statement of profit or loss in a fixed format
- some account names are changed when transferred
- some accounts are grouped together and given a new name

EXAMPLE – new account names and account groupings in the SPL

ITB or ETB account name	New name or grouping in SPL
Sales	Sales revenue or Revenue
Interest paid and bank charges	Finance costs
Cash and Bank	Cash and cash equivalents
Sales ledger control	Trade receivables
Purchases ledger control	Trade payables
NCA original cost less accumulated dep'n	NCA Carrying amount
Wages	Payroll expenses
Various, eg telephone, stationery	Administration expenses
Various, eg advertising, commission paid	Selling expenses
Various, eg carriage out, vehicle expenses	Distribution expenses

further possible combinations of account balances

■ sales account *minus* sales returns account = Revenue

■ purchases account *minus* purchases returns account *plus* carriage inwards = Purchases

STATEMENT OF PROFIT OR LOSS (SPL) – Sole trader format

▇ The format and entries shown on this and the page below are for a sole trader who buys
and sells a product. Note that not all SPLs will have **all** these entries.

The SPL of a sole trader who sells a service rather than a product will have less
detail, eg there will be no Cost of sales section and no gross profit.

Statement of profit of loss for the period ended *(date)*		
	£	£
Sales revenue		A
Opening inventory	B	
Purchases	C	
	D (B+C)	
Less Closing inventory	E	
Cost of sales		F (D minus E)
Gross profit		**G (A minus F)**
Add:		
Discounts received		H
Interest received		I
Gain on disposal of NCA *		J
Allowance for d/d adj: decrease *		K
		L (G + H to K)

Less:		
Administration expenses	M	
Payroll expenses	N	
Selling expenses	O	
Finance costs	P	
Discount allowed	Q	
Depreciation charges	R	
Loss on disposal of NCA *	S	
Irrecoverable debts	T	
Allowance for d/debts adj: increase *	U	
		V (total of M to U)
Profit (loss) for the period		**W (L minus V)**

Notes

The entries with an asterisk (*) show the position of these accounts if they **are** included in the statement of profit or loss. These entries with the asterisk will show:

■ either a gain or a loss on disposal of non-current assets ('NCA'): the **gain** on disposal will be **added** to total profit, the **loss** on disposal will be **deducted**

■ either a decrease or an increase in allowance for doubtful debts ('d/debts adj'): the **decrease** will be **added** to total profit, the **increase** will be **deducted**

EXAMPLE – statement of profit or loss with figures

Note that not all of the accounts or combined accounts shown in the format on the last two pages are included in this example.

This page shows the top half of the statement of profit or loss. The bottom half is shown on the page below.

	Statement of profit of loss for the year ended 31 December 20X4	
	£	£
Sales revenue		345,000
Opening inventory	75,000	
Purchases	201,000	
	276,000	
Less Closing inventory	70,000	
Cost of sales		206,000
Gross profit		**139,000**
Add:		
Discounts received		2,000
		141,000

any returns will already have been deducted from these figures →

gross profit *plus* other income →

Less:		
Administration expenses	24,500	
Payroll expenses	39,000	
Selling expenses	16,000	
Finance costs	1,100	total of expenses
Discount allowed	3,000	
Depreciation charges	7,000	
Loss on disposal of NCA	200	
Irrecoverable debts	500	
Allowance for d/debts adjustment	300	
		91,600
Profit (loss) for the year		49,400

Profit (or loss) for the period is added to (or deducted from) the Capital section in the Statement of financial position (see page 55)

alternative ways of displaying cost of sales in the SPL

1 The common method of displaying the cost of sales in the statement of profit or loss is shown below. In this case the entries shown are the **individual account balances** transferred from the trial balance.

	£	£
Sales revenue		345,000
Opening inventory	75,000	
Purchases	201,000	
	276,000	
Less Closing inventory	70,000	
Cost of sales		206,000
Gross profit		**139,000**

2 An alternative method of displaying the cost of sales in the statement of profit or loss is used when there is a **cost of sales account** in the trial balance. This makes the transfer to the statement of profit or loss much simpler, but the downside is that the statement of profit or loss displays less information, eg the change in inventory.

	£	£
Sales revenue		345,000
Cost of sales		206,000
Gross profit		**139,000**

STATEMENT OF FINANCIAL POSITION (SFP) – Sole trader format – a reminder

The format of the SFP reflects the accounting equation: *assets – liabilities = capital*
The SFP calculations are shown on the next two pages and an example on pages 54-55.

ASSETS

non-current assets:
Items bought for use within the business which have a useful life of more than a year, eg machinery, vehicles, furniture, equipment. These are classified as **tangible** (having material substance, touchable) or **intangible** (not touchable), eg goodwill, trademarks.

current assets:
Items needed for everyday use within the business that will be used or will change within a year, eg inventory, trade receivables, money. Also includes the value of prepaid expenses and accrued income.

minus

LIABILITIES

non-current liabilities:
Long-term debts repayable beyond one year, eg bank loans, mortgages.

current liabilities:
Short-term debt repayable within a year, eg trade payables, bank overdraft, VAT and payroll taxes due to HMRC. Also includes prepaid income and accrued expenses.

equals

CAPITAL

Investment by the owner(s) and therefore a liability of the business. Calculated as opening capital *plus* profit *minus* drawings.

statement of financial position (sole trader): calculations needed

Non-current assets	Cost	Accumulated depreciation	Carrying amount
Asset grouping, eg machinery	A	B	C (A minus B)
Current assets			
Inventory		D	
Trade receivables	E		
Less allowance for doubtful debts	F		
		G (E minus F)	
Prepayment of expenses		H	
Accruals of income		I	
Cash and cash equivalents		J	
		K (total D + G to J)	
Less current liabilities			
Trade payables	L		
Accruals of expenses	M		
Prepayment of income	N		
VAT	O		
Bank overdraft (if not in current assets)	P		
		Q (total L to P)	
Net current assets			R (K minus Q)

Less Non-current liabilities			
Loan			S
NET ASSETS			**T** **(C + R minus S)**
FINANCED BY			
Capital			
Opening capital			U
Add profit (loss) for the period			V
			W (U+V)
Less drawings			X
Closing capital			**Y (W + X)**

The values at T and Y should be the same.
The SFP balances.
The accounting equation is proved:
assets – liabilities = capital

EXAMPLE – statement of financial position (sole trader) with sample figures

Statement of financial position as at 30 September 20X3			
Non-current assets	Cost	Accumulated depreciation	Carrying amount
	£	£	£
Machinery	36,000	14,000	22,000
Current assets			
Inventory		70,000	
Trade receivables	30,000		
Less allowance for doubtful debts	500		
		29,500	
Prepayment of expenses		1,000	
Cash and cash equivalents		9,900	
		110,400	
Less current liabilities			
Trade payables	20,000		
Accruals of expenses	1,500		
VAT	16,000		
		37,500	
Net current assets			72,900

Less Non-current liabilities			
Loan			21,500
NET ASSETS			**73,400**
FINANCED BY			
Capital			
Opening capital			45,000
Add profit (loss) for the period (from SPL)			49,400
			94,400
Less drawings			21,000
Closing capital			**73,400**

This is the profit figure transferred from the statement of profit or loss (see page 49).

Drawings are not an expense but a reduction in capital for sole trader statements.

6 Partnerships – capital and current accounts

INTRODUCTION

A partnership is an unincorporated business owned and run by more than one individual. Profits are shared between the partners who may number from two to twenty or more.

A partnership, like a sole trader, presents its accounts in a statement of profit or loss and a statement of financial position.

The **Partnership Act 1890**, which regulates the way a partnership operates, describes a partnership as 'persons carrying on a business in common with a view to profit'. The terms of the Act can be added to by a written **partnership agreement** which regulates:

- the way profits are divided between partners (by percentage, fraction or ratio)
- whether any partners are entitled to a salary
- interest paid **to** partners on their capital invested, or paid **by** partners on drawings

If there is no partnership agreement the terms of The Partnership Act will always apply. There is more on the Partnership Act and partnership agreements on page 69.

how do partnership accounts differ from sole trader accounts?

Sole trader	Partnership	Partnership accounts treatment
Capital account	Capital accounts for a partner	Capital invested by a partner in the partnership business
Drawings account	Current accounts for each partner	Used to enter partner drawings, salary, interest and profit share
SPL bottom line is net profit owed to the owner	SPL bottom line is profit owed to partners	An Appropriation account is added to the end of the SPL giving details of the division of the profit
SFP Financed by section = Opening capital plus profits less drawings	SFP Financed by section = end of period balances of partners' Capital and Current accounts	Profit share is included in the current account entries
Sole trader stops trading	Partnership carries on: partner leaves, joins or profit share is altered	A value is put on the business in addition to the value shown in the SFP. Goodwill is created for partners

Capital account – the value of the partner's investment

A capital account for a partner is like the capital account of a sole trader. It records any capital introduced or added during the partner's service but otherwise remains untouched.

EXAMPLE

Peter Artner joins a partnership on 1 January 20X0 and introduces £20,000 of capital. In July 20X5 he contributes additional capital of £10,000. The partnership year-end is 31 December. He leaves the partnership on 30 September 20X8.

Capital account: P Artner					
			1 Jan 20X0	Bank	20,000
31 Dec 20X5	Balance c/d	30,000	1 Jul 20X5	Bank	10,000
		30,000			30,000
30 Sep 20X8	Bank	30,000	1 Jan 20X6	Balance b/d	30,000

On 30 Sep 20X8, the partnership pays back Peter's total capital contribution of £30,000

From 1 Jan 20X0 to 30 June 20X5, the partnership owes Peter £20,000

From 1 Jul 20X5 to 30 Sep 20X8, the partnership owes Peter a total of £30,000 (£20,000 + £10,000)

Current account – where most of the action happens

EXAMPLE

For the year ending 31 December 20X6, Peter Artner's current account included the entries listed below. Note that the figures (b) to (f) are totals – in reality there would be more and smaller entries in the account. The current account is also shown below.

1 Jan 20X6	(a)	Balance brought down	£15,000
31 Dec 20X6	(b)	Total salary paid during year	£12,000
	(c)	Total drawings during the year	£25,000
	(d)	Interest on capital	£1,500
	(e)	Interest on drawings	£500
	(f)	Profit share	£20,000

	Current account: P Artner					
31 Dec X6	(c) Drawings	25,000	1 Jan X6	(a) Bal b/d	15,000
31 Dec X6	(e) Int on drawings	500	31 Dec X6	(b) Bank - Salary	12,000
31 Dec X6	Balance c/d	23,000	31 Dec X6	(d) Interest on capital	1,500
			31 Dec X6	(f) Profit share	20,000
		48,500			48,500
			1 Jan X7	Balance b/d	23,000

7 Partnerships – goodwill

WHAT IS GOODWILL?

Goodwill is the difference between the market value of a business and the value in its accounts of its separate assets and liabilities (its 'net' value).

If the net assets of a partnership in its statement of financial position (SFP) are £100,000 but the business is valued at £150,000 (ie what an outsider might be prepared to pay for it), the goodwill is worth £50,000.

Goodwill does not appear in the financial statements of a partnership.

when is goodwill relevant to a partnership?

Goodwill is used to reward existing partners for their input into the business by paying them their share of the value of goodwill when there is a change in the partnership, eg

- on admission of a new partner
- on departure of an existing partner (through leaving, retirement or death)
- when there is a change in profit share

These changes may happen part way through a financial year.

how is goodwill valued?

Goodwill is usually based on the average profits of the business over the previous few years.

what is the double-entry for goodwill?

- the double-entry occurs when there is a change in the partnership, eg new partner joining, existing partner leaving, or change in allocation of profits between partners
- goodwill has its own T account
- goodwill is an intangible asset
- the goodwill value is very short-lived in the partnership accounts: the asset is created and written off (eliminated) at the same time – the 'other' entry of the double-entry is in the partners' capital accounts:

creation of goodwill	
debit	Goodwill account
credit	partners' capital accounts in **old** profit-sharing ratios

elimination of goodwill	
debit	partners' capital accounts in **new** profit-sharing ratios
credit	Goodwill account

Remember that goodwill does not appear in the financial statements of a partnership.

EXAMPLE 1 – Mal, Luke and Liz: introduction of a new partner

■ Mal and Luke run an expanding travel agency partnership, sharing profits equally.

■ They admit a new partner, Liz, on 1 October 20X4. Goodwill is valued at £50,000.

■ The new partnership agreement states that profits are to be shared as follows: 40% (Mal), 40% (Luke) and 20% (Liz).

■ Liz brings £25,000 in capital to the business; Mal and Luke have balances in their capital accounts of £30,000 each.

Goodwill					
1 Oct X4	(a) Capital Mal (50%)	25,000	1 Oct X4	(c) Capital Mal (40%)	20,000
1 Oct X4	(b) Capital Luke (50%)	25,000	1 Oct X4	(d) Capital Luke (40%)	20,000
			1 Oct X4	(e) Capital Liz (20%)	10,000
		50,000			50,000

Note that these partnership profit shares can be expressed in different ways:

■ **percentages**: 40%, 40% and 20% as shown above, or

■ **fractions**: 2/5, 2/5 and 1/5 (two fifths, two fifths and one fifth), or

■ **a ratio**: 2:2:1

extracts from the three partners' capital accounts

Capital: Mal	
(c) 20,000	b/d 30,000
c/d 35,000	(a) 25,000
55,000	55,000
	b/d 35,000

Capital: Luke	
(d) 20,000	b/d 30,000
c/d 35,000	(b) 25,000
55,000	55,000
	b/d 35,000

Capital: Liz	
(e) 10,000	25,000
c/d 15,000	
25,000	25,000
	b/d 15,000

■ **Liz's** capital account shows her contribution of £25,000 (Cr) on joining the partnership.

The balance is immediately reduced by £10,000 (Dr), payment for her 20% of the goodwill of the business, ie £50,000 x 20% = £10,000.

20% is her agreed share in the new partnership.

■ The capital account balances of the existing partners – **Mal** and **Luke** – have increased from £30,000 to £35,000.

This extra £5,000 each is their half share of Liz's payment (£10,000) for joining their successful partnership.

Their agreed share in the new partnership is now 40% (reduced from 50%).

journal entries for the creation of goodwill

Date	Account	Dr	Cr
1 Oct 20X4	Goodwill	50,000	
	Capital Mal		25,000
	Capital Luke		25,000
	Goodwill created on admission of new partner		

Goodwill created

old profit-sharing ratios (50:50)

journal entries for the elimination of goodwill

Date	Account	Dr	Cr
1 Oct 20X4	Capital Mal	20,000	
	Capital Luke	20,000	
	Capital Liz	10,000	
	Goodwill		50,000
	Goodwill eliminated on admission of new partner		

new profit-sharing ratios (40:40:20)

Goodwill created

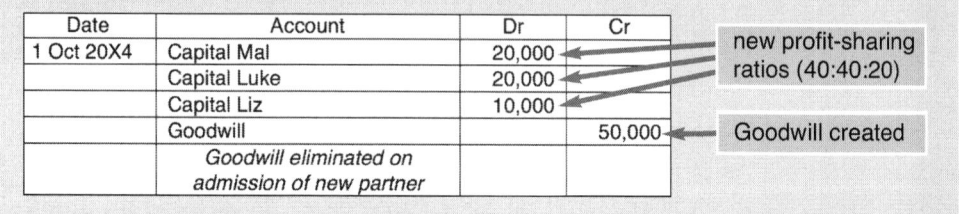

EXAMPLE 2 – Cate, Dave and Lars: retirement of a partner

■ Cate, Dave and Lars have been running a successful software development partnership for many years, sharing profits equally (in thirds).

■ Dave retired on 31 July 20X4.

■ Goodwill is valued at £90,000.

■ The partners' capital accounts before Dave's retirement all show a balance of £40,000.

■ The new partnership agreement states that profits are to be shared equally between the remaining partners, Cate and Lars.

The Goodwill account appears as follows:

	Goodwill				
	Creation			Elimination	
31 Jul X4	(a) Capital Cate (1/3)	30,000	31 Jul X4	(d) Capital Cate (1/2)	45,000
31 Jul X4	(b) Capital Dave (1/3)	30,000	31 Jul X4	(e) Capital Lars (1/2)	45,000
31 Jul X4	(c) Capital Lars (1/3)	30,000			
		90,000			90,000

extracts from the capital accounts on Dave's retirement:

Capital: Cate	
(d) 45,000	b/d 40,000
c/d 25,000	(a) 30,000
70,000	70,000
	b/d 25,000

Capital: Dave	
Bank 70,000	b/d 40,000
	(b) 30,000
70,000	70,000

Capital: Lars	
(e) 45,000	b/d 40,000
c/d 25,000	(c) 30,000
70,000	70,000
	b/d 25,000

- The capital account balances of the remaining partners – Cate and Lars – have reduced from £40,000 to £25,000.

- Cate and Lars have paid to Dave their shares of Dave's goodwill which is due to him on leaving the partnership. Dave's goodwill is £30,000 (one third of £90,000), so Cate and Lars each pay £15,000.

- Dave has received a bank payment for £70,000 on retirement.

  This is made up of his Capital account balance (£40,000) plus his share of the goodwill as at 31 July 20X4 (£30,000).

alternative scenario: what if Dave had left £50,000 in the business as a loan?

Instead of taking all his money out of the partnership on his retirement, Dave might have left some capital in the business as a loan, say £50,000.

This would help Cate and Lars to carry the business on as a going concern, but Dave would be free of all liability for the partnership.

In this case:

■ The debit entry in Dave's Capital account would have been split between the amount paid to him (£20,000) and the amount transferred to a separate loan account (£50,000). Dave's Capital account will appear as follows:

Capital: Dave			
Bank	20,000	b/d	40,000
Loan	50,000	(b)	30,000
	70,000		70,000

■ Note that whether Dave leaves money in the business as a loan or takes out the full amount, his Capital account will be reduced to zero once he has retired from the partnership.

8 Partnerships – appropriation account

DISTRIBUTING THE PROFIT

A partnership statement of profit or loss is in principle much the same as that of a sole trader. But one major difference is the use of a separate Appropriation account which follows on from the profit figure at the bottom of the normal statement of profit or loss.

The Appropriation account is essentially a calculation of what each partner is to be paid at the end of an accounting period.

calculations in the Appropriation account

	profit (or loss) for the year from the statement of profit or loss
plus	**interest** charged on partners' drawings
minus	**deductions from profit** (salaries paid to partners, interest on capital)
equals	**profit (or loss) to be shared between the partners**

details of the calculations in the Appropriation account

The calculation of the profit (or loss) **for each partner** in the Appropriation account (which follows on from the statement of profit or loss) is:

> **Profit (or loss)** for the year from the statement of profit or loss; this 'bottom line' total is always the starting point for the Appropriation account.

plus **Interest on partners' drawings charged to the partners** if they withdraw drawings earlier than normal; this is a form of borrowing and the interest rate will be set by the partnership agreement. This interest is added to the profit due to the partners.

minus **Salaries of partners**: some partners take a salary as well as a share of profit – these have to be authorised in the partnership agreement and will reduce profit.

minus **Interest allowed on capital**: interest paid to partners is compensation for the capital they have invested – this is calculated by multiplying the capital account balances by an agreed percentage set out in the partnership agreement, either at the beginning or at the end of the period.

equals **Profit or loss to be shared between the partners**: this is the final figure of profit or loss for the individual partners. The percentages will normally be set out in the partnership agreement; if they are not, the Partnership Act requires the profit or loss to be shared equally.

Appropriation account – format showing calculation formulas

This shows the Appropriation account set out just below the statement of profit or loss. The figure G represents the profit and figures H to M represent the Appropriation account.

SPL	Profit for period			G
	Add interest on drawings	Partner 1	H	
		Partner 2	H	Total H
				L (G + H)
	Less appropriation of profit:			
Appropriation account	Salaries	Partner 1	I	
		Partner 2	I	Total I
	Interest on capital	Partner 1	J	
		Partner 2	J	Total J
	Profit available for distribution			M (L - I - J)
	Profit share	Partner 1	K	
		Partner 2	K	
	Total profit distributed			M

EXAMPLE – Appropriation account with figures

Here the bottom line from a partnership statement of profit or loss shows profit available of £74,000, ready to be distributed and apportioned in the appropriation account below.

SPL	**Profit (loss) for the period**			**74,000**

Appropriation account				
Add interest on drawings	Partner 1		450	
	Partner 2		550	1,000
				75,000
Less appropriation of profit:				
Salaries	Partner 1		-	
	Partner 2		15,000	15,000
Interest on capital (5%)	Partner 1		1,700	
	Partner 2		1,300	3,000
Profit available for distribution				57,000
Profit share	Partner 1 (60%)	34,200		
	Partner 2 (40%)	22,800		
Total profit distributed				57,000

9 Partnerships – changes during the year

WHAT HAPPENS WHEN THE PARTNERSHIP CHANGES?

There are various changes that can take place within a partnership during the financial year and in each case the accounting system will need to be adjusted. The changes that can take place include changes of partners and changes in profit allocation.

The main record that will need adjustment will be the Appropriation account – see the last chapter for an explanation of its workings.

what are the main changes?

The main changes that you will know how to deal with are:

■ partners joining the partnership during the year

■ partners leaving the partnership during the year

■ changes in profit-sharing ratios during the year

In each case of 'split' years – ie changes in the partnership during the year – there will be different accounting treatments in each part of the year.

treatment of changes in the Appropriation account

What if there are changes in the partnership structure during the financial year?

The Appropriation account will be expanded as follows (extract shown here):

Partnership appropriation account for the period ended 30 June 20X4		1 Jul-31 Dec X3	1 Jan-30 Jun X4	
Profit for period		50,225	50,225	100,450
Add interest on drawings	Partner 1	225	225	450
	Partner 2	275	275	550
	Partner 3	-	250	250
		50,725	50,975	101,700

separate columns for the divisions of the year   new total column

Note the following:

▪ each part of the divided year is given a separate column in the Appropriation account

▪ there is an additional column added on the right-hand side of the account which totals the divisions of the year

▪ the division of the year may be in any number of months, eg 6 and 6, 3 and 9 months (obviously they have to add up to 12)

calculation and apportionment of figures for the Appropriation account

In order to complete the Appropriation account you will have to calculate the figures to go in the various columns. These will relate to the proportional 'split' between the total figures for the year. You are likely to have to:

■ apportion the profit from the SPL to each part of the year

■ apportion interest on drawings to each part of the year and to each partner

■ apportion salaries to each part of the year and to relevant partners

■ apportion interest on capital to each part of the year and to each partner

■ apportion profit share to each part of the year and to each partner according to their shares in each period

EXAMPLE – apportionment of a partner's salary over 12 months

A salary of £18,000 p.a. has to be apportioned into a 3 month and a 9 month period:

3 months salary = £18,000 x 3/12 = £4,500

9 months salary = £18,000 x 9/12 = £13,500

Now study the three examples that follow showing the treatments of profit-sharing ratios changing, partners joining and partners leaving during the course of a year.

EXAMPLE 1 – change in profit-sharing ratio from 1 January 20X4

Partners 1 and 2 shared profits 60/40 to 31 December 20X3 and 50/50 from 1 January 20X4.

Partnership appropriation account for the period ended 30 June 20X4				
		1 Jul-31 Dec X3	1 Jan-30 Jun X4	
Profit for period		37,000	37,000	74,000
Add interest on drawings	Partner 1	225	225	450
	Partner 2	275	275	550
		37,500	37,500	75,000
Less appropriation of profit:				
Salaries	Partner 1	-	-	-
	Partner 2	7,500	7,500	15,000
Interest on capital (5%)	Partner 1	850	850	1,700
	Partner 2	650	650	1,300
Profit available for distribution		28,500	28,500	57,000
Profit share	Part 1	(60%) 17,100	(50%) 14,250	31,350
	Part 2	(40%) 11,400	(50%) 14,250	25,650
Total profit distributed		28,500	28,500	57,000

EXAMPLE 2 – new partner joining on 1 January 20X4

Partners 1 and 2 shared profits 60/40 to 31 December 20X3. Partner 3 joined on 1 January 20X4 and the new profit-sharing ratio is one third each. Partner 3 is entitled to annual salary of £16,000.

Partnership appropriation account for the period ended 30 June 20X4				
		1 Jul-31 Dec X3	1 Jan-30 Jun X4	
Profit for period		50,225	50,225	100,450
Add interest on drawings	Partner 1	225	225	450
	Partner 2	275	275	550
	Partner 3	-	250	250
		50,725	50,975	101,700
Less appropriation of profit:				
Salaries	Partner 1	-	-	-
	Partner 2	7,500	7,500	15,000
	Partner 3	-	8,000	8,000
Interest on capital (5%)	Partner 1	850	850	1,700
	Partner 2	650	650	1,300
	Partner 3	-	975	975
Profit available for distribution		41,725	33,000	74,725
Profit share	Partner 1	(60%) 25,035	(33.3%) 11,000	36,035
	Partner 2	(40%) 16,690	(33.3%) 11,000	27,690
	Partner 3	-	(33.3%) 11,000	11,000
Total profit distributed		41,725	33,000	74,725

EXAMPLE 3 – a partner leaves on 31 December 20X4

Partners 1, 2 and 3 shared profits equally to 31 December 20X4. Partner 1 retires, leaving partners 2 and 3 to share profits 60/40 respectively from 1 January 20X5.

Partnership appropriation account for the period ended 30 June 20X5				
		1 Jul-31 Dec X4	1 Jan-30 Jun X5	
Profit for period		49,075	49,075	98,150
Add interest on drawings	Partner 1	250	-	250
	Partner 2	300	300	600
	Partner 3	350	350	700
		49,975	49,725	99,700
Less appropriation of profit:				
Salaries	Partner 1	-	-	
	Partner 2	8,000	8,000	16,000
	Partner 3	10,000	10,000	20,000
Interest on capital (5%)	Partner 1	575	-	575
	Partner 2	750	750	1,500
	Partner 3	650	650	1,300
Profit available for distribution		30,000	30,325	60,325
Profit share	Partner 1	(1/3) 10,000	-	10,000
	Partner 2	(1/3) 10,000	(60%) 18,195	28,195
	Partner 3	(1/3) 10,000	(40%) 12,130	22,130
Total profit distributed		30,000	30,325	60,325

10 Partnerships – statement of financial position

FORMAT DIFFERENCES

A partnership Statement of financial position follows the same format as that of a sole trader down to and including the 'Net assets' line.

The 'Financed by' section which follows is very different.

This is explained and illustrated on the pages that follow.

what are the main changes in the 'Financed by' section?

- it shows the partners' current and capital accounts at the end of the financial period (instead of the sole trader's '*capital + profit – drawings = closing capital*' calculation)

- it displays the partners' current and capital account balances listed individually, either in a horizontal format or, if there are many partners, in a vertical format

- it contains no profit or profit calculation (it has all been allocated to the current accounts via the Appropriation account)

'Financed by' section of SFP – partners listed horizontally, accounts vertically

This extract from a partnership statement of financial position shows the balances of **two** partners' capital and current accounts.

- the partners are listed horizontally in a row; their account totals are in the bottom row
- the capital and current accounts are listed vertically; their account totals are in the right-hand column

FINANCED BY			
	Partner 1 (£)	**Partner 2 (£)**	**£**
Capital accounts	Capital Account	Capital Account	**Total**
Current accounts	Current Account	Current Account	**Total**
	Total for Partner 1	**Total for Partner 2**	**Total**

this total should agree with the net assets total on the 'top' part of the SFP

there are separate columns for each of the two partners showing the total money share they have in the partnership – note that it is possible that the current account may have a negative balance, in which case it will be shown in brackets

EXAMPLE – a complete partnership SFP – with figures

Statement of financial position as at 31 March 20X4			
Non-current assets	Cost	Accumulated depreciation	Carrying amount
	£	£	£
Equipment	46,800	18,200	28,600
Current assets			
Inventory		91,000	
Trade receivables	39,000		
Less allowance for doubtful debts	600		
		38,400	
Prepayment of expenses		1,300	
Cash and cash equivalents		12,900	
		143,600	
Less current liabilities			
Trade payables	26,000		
Accruals of expenses	1,900		
VAT	20,800		
		48,700	
Net current assets			94,900

Less Non-current liabilities			
Loan			28,000
NET ASSETS			**95,500**
FINANCED BY			
	Partner 1	Partner 2	
Capital accounts	25,000	30,000	55,000
Current accounts	19,000	21,500	40,500
Totals	44,000	51,500	**95,500**

profits have already been allocated to the current accounts, so there is no profit figure in the 'Financed by' section of the statement of profit or loss

On the next two pages there is an example of an alternative way of setting out the statement of financial position, with the partners listed vertically rather than in a row.

'Financed by' section of SFP – partners listed vertically

This format is likely to be used when there are 3 or more partners and so it becomes impractical to list them horizontally in a row as there will not be enough space.

The solution is to list the partners and the account balances in two vertical columns.

The format is shown below and an example with figures on the next page.

FINANCED BY		
Capital accounts:		
Partner 1	Capital account	
Partner 2	Capital account	
Partner 3	Capital account	
		Total of Capital accounts
Current accounts:		
Partner 1	(Current account)	
Partner 2	Current account	
Partner 3	Current account	
		Total of Current accounts
		Total of Capital and Current accounts

if a partner's current account has a debit balance, it is shown in brackets and deducted from the other figures

EXAMPLE – 'Financed by' section of SFP: partners listed vertically – with figures

Net assets		114,000
FINANCED BY		
Capital accounts:		
Partner 1	30,000	
Partner 2	25,000	
Partner 3	35,000	
		90,000
Current accounts:		
Partner 1	(5,000)	
Partner 2	14,000	
Partner 3	15,000	
		24,000
		114,000

11 Memory aids

KEEPING YOUR MEMORY FIT

The human brain is an odd organ – you can remember the most useless facts, but when it comes to complex matters such as accounting procedures the mind can go completely blank. But it is possible to train your brain.

At the beginning of this Guide there are some revision tips which suggest that you can study effectively and recall information by . . .

- **Observing**, *ie remembering what information looks like on the page, using diagrams, lists, mind-maps and colour coding. Memory is very visual.*

- **Writing** *information down, using flash cards, post-it notes, notes on a phone. It is the actual process of writing which helps to fix the information in the brain.*

- **Learning** *by regularly going through your course notes and text books. Find a 'study buddy' in your class (or online) to teach and test each other as the course progresses.*

- **Chill out** *when you get tired. Give your brain a chance to recover. Get some exercise and fresh air, work out. In the ancient world there was the saying that a fit body was usually home to a fit mind.*

- **Treats** *– promise yourself rewards when you have finished studying – meet friends, eat chocolate, have a drink, listen to music.*

exam preparation

- **Practice, practice, practice** *when preparing for your assessment.*

  Practice the questions and assessments in the Osborne Books workbooks.

  Practice the free online assessments on the Osborne Books website:

  Go to www.osbornebooks.co.uk/aat_accounting_qcf *or scan this code . . . .*

using the memory aids

On the next few pages are blank spaces for you to set out ways of remembering many of the definitions and formulas needed for your AAT assessment.

PERIOD-END ADJUSTMENTS

Complete the table below stating how both the statement of profit or loss and the statement of financial position are affected by period-end adjustments. The first two entries have been made for you to give an idea of what is required.

adjustment	statement of profit or loss	statement of financial position
accrual of income	add to income	show as current asset
accrual of expense	add to expense	show as current liability
prepayment of income		
irrecoverable debt		
depreciation charge		
goods for owner's use		

USING EQUATIONS TO CALCULATE MISSING FIGURES

Complete the right-hand column of the table below setting out the equation you would use to calculate the value listed in the left-hand column.

missing figure	equation you would use to calculate the missing figure
assets (from liabilities and capital)	
capital (from assets and liabilities)	
drawings (from opening capital, profit and closing capital)	
sales revenue (from cost of sales, and known mark-up %)	

ENTRIES IN A PARTNER'S CURRENT ACCOUNT

Write down on the correct sides of the account the entries you would expect to find in a partners' current account.

debit	A Partner – current account	credit

ENTRIES FOR THE CREATION AND ELIMINATION OF GOODWILL

Write 'debit' or 'credit' in the right-hand column of the table below to indicate if the accounts for the **creation** of goodwill in a partnership have a debit or a credit entry.

account name	debit or credit?
Goodwill account	
Partner capital account	

Write 'debit' or 'credit' in the right-hand column of the table below to indicate if the accounts for the **elimination** of goodwill in a partnership have a debit or a credit entry.

account name	debit or credit?
Goodwill account	
Partner capital account	

index

index

for your notes